BENTLEY
CONTINENTAL GT

BY CALVIN CRUZ

BELLWETHER MEDIA • MINNEAPOLIS, MN

TM

Are you ready to take it to the extreme?
Torque books thrust you into the action-packed world
of sports, vehicles, mystery, and adventure. These books
may include dirt, smoke, fire, and dangerous stunts.
WARNING: read at your own risk.

This edition first published in 2016 by Bellwether Media, Inc.

No part of this publication may be reproduced in whole or in part without written permission of the publisher.
For information regarding permission, write to Bellwether Media, Inc., Attention: Permissions Department,
5357 Penn Avenue South, Minneapolis, MN 55419.

Library of Congress Cataloging-in-Publication Data

Cruz, Calvin, author.
  Bentley Continental GT / by Calvin Cruz.
    pages cm -- (Torque. Car crazy)
  Summary: "Engaging images accompany information about the Bentley Continental GT. The combination
of high-interest subject matter and light text is intended for students in grades 3 through 7"--Provided by
publisher.
  Includes bibliographical references and index.
  Audience: 7-12.
  Audience: Grades 3-7.
  ISBN 978-1-62617-278-4 (hardcover : alk. paper)
  1. Bentley automobile--Juvenile literature. I. Title.
  TL215.B4C78 2016
  629.222'2--dc23
                                    2015004218

Printed in the United States of America, North Mankato, MN.

TABLE OF CONTENTS

SPEED, COMFORT, AND STYLE

A driver gets into his Bentley Continental GT. He adjusts the **bucket seat** and puts on his sunglasses. The driver presses a start button and the engine rumbles to life. He checks his mirrors and pulls out onto the road.

The road is empty ahead of the Continental GT. The driver pushes the pedal to the floor. The engine roars with power as the car cruises down the road. The driver enjoys the smooth ride in his **supercar**. He relaxes in the **luxury** of his Bentley.

ALL IN A NAME
THE GT STANDS FOR "GRAND TOURER."

THE HISTORY OF BENTLEY

Walter Owen Bentley

Bentley Motors was formed by Walter Owen Bentley in 1919. Walter was an English **engineer** who had worked on **locomotives** and airplane engines. He also sold French cars before World War I. But he had dreams of selling his own cars.

Walter put many of his early cars into racing. He knew that finishing well in races would increase sales. Bentley cars won the **24 Hours of Le Mans** five times between 1924 and 1930. They also set many speed records. Walter's plan worked. Bentley cars were a hit!

24 Hours of Le Mans

1925 Bentley 3-Litre Speed

However, Bentley sales soon began to slow. People could not afford expensive cars during the **Great Depression**. The company struggled to make money. It was sold to Rolls-Royce.

Bentley R-Type Continental

BACK IN ACTION

BENTLEY COMPETED AGAIN IN THE 24 HOURS OF LE MANS IN 2001. THE COMPANY HAD NOT BEEN IN THE RACE FOR MORE THAN 70 YEARS. IN 2003, THE BENTLEY SPEED 8 WON.

In 1998, the Volkswagen Group bought the company. Since then, Bentley has come out with many popular **models**. They are fan favorites once again!

BENTLEY CONTINENTAL GT

The first Bentley Continental GT came out in 2003. It was designed for driving fast in comfort and style. Today there are several kinds of Continental GTs. Some have more powerful engines. Others offer more comfort. Each edition can be a **coupe** or a **convertible**.

Bentley Continental GT V8 S Convertible

Bentley
Continental GT
Speed

TAKE YOUR PICK
THE DIFFERENT CONTINENTAL GT
OPTIONS ARE THE GT V8, GT V8 S,
GT W12, AND GT SPEED.

Bentley Continental GT
V8 Coupe

TECHNOLOGY AND GEAR

Different options and attention to detail keep all Continental GT drivers happy. Drivers can choose between two kinds of engines. The **V8 engine** performs well, and the **W12 engine** has extra power. Both engines are designed to use as little fuel as possible. All-wheel drive helps the cars grip the road in any condition.

W12 engine

FOR THE RECORD

IN 2007, A CONTINENTAL GT BROKE THE SPEED RECORD ON ICE. IT REACHED 199.83 MILES (321.60 KILOMETERS) PER HOUR!

The **interior** is built to offer a quiet ride for a comfortable experience. A mix of wood, leather, and chrome gives the car a classy feel. Continental GT owners can choose the color of the car's paint and interior.

The front seats and steering wheel can be heated to keep drivers and passengers warm in cold weather. Air vents beneath the headrests also blow warm air. **Massage** settings in the front seats relax riders during long drives.

Continental GTs also have the newest technology. The sound system can store thousands of songs. Eleven speakers offer top-notch sound quality. The car can even be set up to offer Internet!

2015 BENTLEY CONTINENTAL GT SPECIFICATIONS

CAR STYLE	COUPE OR CONVERTIBLE
ENGINE	6.0L W12
TOP SPEED	198 MILES (319 KILOMETERS) PER HOUR
0 – 60 TIME	4.3 SECONDS
HORSEPOWER	582 HP (434 KILOWATTS) @ 6100 RPM
CURB WEIGHT	5,115 POUNDS (2,320 KILOGRAMS)
WIDTH	87.6 INCHES (223 CENTIMETERS)
LENGTH	189.3 INCHES (481 CENTIMETERS)
HEIGHT	55.2 INCHES (140 CENTIMETERS)
WHEEL SIZE	20 INCHES (51 CENTIMETERS)
COST	STARTS AROUND $210,000

TODAY AND THE FUTURE

The Bentley Continental GT gives drivers a balance of power and comfort. The car has been popular since it came out. It has won many awards for its design and performance. The Continental GT continues to be popular for drivers who want a luxury experience from their supercar!

GRAND CHAMPION
THE BENTLEY CONTINENTAL GT WON THE GRAND TOURER OF THE YEAR AWARD FROM *TOP GEAR* IN 2010.

SMOOTH BODY LINES

LARGE GRILLE

FOUR HEADLIGHTS

GLOSSARY

24 Hours of Le Mans—a race in which a team of drivers competes for 24 hours

bucket seat—a seat with a rounded back to keep a person in place when turning at high speeds

convertible—a car with a folding or soft roof

coupe—a car with a hard roof and two doors

engineer—a person who designs and builds cars and other machines

Great Depression—a period of time from the late 1920s through the 1930s when people did not have a lot of money

interior—the inside of a car

locomotives—railroad vehicles that pull train cars

luxury—expensive and offering great comfort

massage—to rub muscles to relax

models—specific kinds of cars

supercar—an expensive and high-performing sports car

V8 engine—an engine with 8 cylinders arranged in the shape of a "V"

W12 engine—an engine with 12 cylinders arranged in the shape of a "W"

TO LEARN MORE

AT THE LIBRARY

Colson, Rob. *Luxury Cars*. London, U.K.: Wayland, 2015.

Gifford, Clive. *Car Crazy*. New York, N.Y.: DK Publishing, 2012.

Kenney, Karen Latchana. *Thrilling Sports Cars*. North Mankato, Minn.: Capstone Press, 2015.

ON THE WEB

Learning more about the Bentley Continental GT is as easy as 1, 2, 3.

1. Go to www.factsurfer.com.

2. Enter "Bentley Continental GT" into the search box.

3. Click the "Surf" button and you will see a list of related web sites.

With factsurfer.com, finding more information is just a click away.

INDEX

The images in this book are reproduced through the courtesy of: PHOTOPQR/ L''ALSACE/ Newscom, front cover; Trainstock/ Superstock, p. 4; Bentley Motors, pp. 4-5, 6-7, 12-13, 14-15, 16-17, 18-19, 20-21; National Motor Museum/ Glow Images, p. 8; Heritage Images/ Corbis, p. 9 (top); DeepGreen, p. 9 (bottom); Pavel L Photo and Video, p. 10; Bocman1973, p. 10 (top left); JuliusKielaitis, p. 10 (top right); Andre Durand/ Getty Images, p. 11.